THE SPACE SHUTTLE

A TRUE BOOK

by

Allison Lassieur

Children's Press®

A Division of Scholastic Inc.

New York Toronto London Auckland Sydney
Mexico City New Delhi Hong Kong

Danbury, Connecticut

A crawler transporter takes the Space Shuttle *Discovery* to be repaired.

Content Consultant
Peter Goodwin
Kent School
Kent, CT

Reading Consultant
Linda Cornwell
Learning Resource
Consultant
Indiana Department
of Education

The photograph on the cover shows a Space Shuttle being launched. The photograph on the title page shows the Space Shuttle Discovery *coming in for a landing at Edwards Air Force Base in California.*

Library of Congress Cataloging-in-Publication Data

Lassieur, Allison
    The space shuttle / by Allison Lassieur.
        p. cm. — (A true book)
    Includes bibliographical references and index.
    Summary: Describes the beginnings of the space shuttle program, the layout of a shuttle, the *Challenger* disaster, and the role of a shuttle in building a space station.
    ISBN: 0-516-22003-9 (lib. bdg.)   0-516-27187-3 (pbk.)
    1. Space shuttles—Juvenile literature. [1. Space shuttles.] I. Title.
II. Series.
TL795.515.L37 2000
629.44'1—dc21   99-055899
                                                            CIP

7 8 9 10 R 09 08 07 06

Contents

This drawing appeared in Jules Verne's book *From the Earth to the Moon.*

Space Shuttle Beginnings

For hundreds of years, people have dreamed of being able to fly into space. In 1865, a man named Jules Verne wrote a book called *From the Earth to the Moon.* He imagined that people would ride on a shuttle train to the Moon and back.

In 1969, the first astronauts landed on the Moon. Soon after, scientists started thinking about building a permanent space station to learn more about space. A space station is a place where people can live and work in space for a long time. Before engineers could design and build a space station, they had to design a reusable spacecraft that could shuttle supplies back and forth between Earth and the station.

Every Space Shuttle has the same design. They look like a cross between an airplane and a rocket.

Engineers tried several shuttle designs. They finally came up with a sleek, black-and-white spacecraft that looks like a cross between an airplane and a rocket. It is 122 feet

This picture of the Space Shuttle *Challenger* in orbit with the payload bay doors open was taken by a camera attached to an astronaut's helmet.

(37 meters) long and has a wingspan of 78 feet (24 m). The United States has built six Space Shuttles, and they all have the same design.

Space Shuttles do not fly all the way to the Moon. They fly in an orbit around Earth, between 190 and 330 miles (306 to 531 kilometers) away.

Name that Shuttle

In 1977, the National Aeronautics and Space Administration (NASA) was about to launch the first shuttle. It was only a test mission that would not go all the way into space, but everyone was excited about it. Scientists named the test shuttle the *Constitution*

Scientists used this Space Shuttle to test how well the new spacecraft would land on Earth.

in honor of an American battleship used during the War of 1812.

The cast of the poplar 1960s television show *Star Trek* was invited to the 1976 dedication ceremony of the Space Shuttle *Enterprise*. From left to right: a NASA official, DeForest Kelly (Dr. Leonard "Bones" McCoy), George Takei (Lieutenant Hikaru Sulu), James Doohan (Lieutenant Commander Montgomery "Scotty" Scott), Nichelle Nichols (Lieutenant Nyota Uhura), Leonard Nimoy (Lieutenant Commander Spock), creator Gene Roddenberry, U.S. Senator Don Fuqua, and Walter Koenig (Ensign Pavel Chekov).

Then NASA started getting a lot of letters. Fans of the television show *Star Trek* wanted the first Space Shuttle to be named after the U.S.S. *Enterprise*, the spaceship on the show. At first NASA ignored the letters, but they kept pouring in. Finally, NASA paid attention. Before the test shuttle's flight, NASA renamed it the *Enterprise*.

The *Enterprise* has now landed for good at the National

Air and Space Museum in Washington, D.C. The Space Shuttle is much too big to be displayed at the museum, so it is in storage. One day, the museum may add a building large enough to display the shuttle and other large spacecraft.

The next five shuttles were named *Columbia, Challenger, Discovery, Atlantis,* and *Endeavor.* They were named after old sailing ships.

Shuttle Parts

- The shuttle is controlled by a pilot on the flight deck.

- Solid rocket boosters and the shuttle's main engines propel it into space.

- Satellites that will be released into space are stored in the payload bay.

- The mid-deck is where the crew lives and works.

Ship Shape

The front end of a Space
Shuttle is round, like the nose
of a rocket. During liftoff,
Space Shuttles are pointed
nose-first toward space and
launched by powerful rocket
motors. The rockets push the
spacecraft up from the ground
and away from Earth.

As Space Shuttle *Discovery* blasts off, the powerful fuel in the fuel tanks pushes the shuttle into space.

The shuttle rides on the back of a huge rocket when it is launched into space. The long, thin tanks on either side are filled with fuel. When the tanks are empty, they drop into the ocean.

When a Space Shuttle lifts off from the ground, it carries a large fuel tank on each side. The fuel is used up during the launch, and then the tanks fall off. The shuttle is always launched from places near the ocean so that the tanks will fall into the water and not on land. The empty tanks float, so they can be picked up and used again.

When the shuttle orbits Earth, it sometimes looks like

The Space Shuttle was designed to glide back to Earth from space. Here, the Space Shuttle *Enterprise* lands during a test.

an airplane flying upside down. Its black underside faces toward space and its white top faces toward Earth.

Space Shuttle orbiters, without the fuel tanks and solid rocket boosters, are shaped so that they can glide back to Earth like an airplane. Even though Space Shuttles land like airplanes, they do not land at regular airports. They need a lot more space than airplanes do.

Hot Stuff

A Space Shuttle cannot be used over again if it is damaged during flight. Scientists had to keep this in mind when they designed the shuttle. They were worried the shuttles might overheat and burn up as they flew back through Earth's atmosphere.

Try rubbing your hands together really fast. Can you feel the heat? A Space Shuttle also gets hot when it flies through the layer of air that surrounds Earth. It rubs against the air and gets very hot. To protect the shuttles, scientists cover them with a special layer of tiles.

Special heat-resistant tiles cover the surface of every Space Shuttle. The material (inset) used to make the shuttle's tiles can withstand bursts of intense heat.

Inside a Space Shuttle

While a Space Shuttle is flying in an orbit around Earth, astronauts have many jobs to do. There is not much room inside a Space Shuttle, but the astronauts stay comfortable. Up to ten astronauts can fit on a Space Shuttle.

These astronauts are preparing for a training mission on the Space Shuttle *Atlantis*.

These controls are used to fly the shuttle, operate the robot arm, and run almost everything on the Space Shuttle.

The cabin inside the shuttle has two levels. The pilot flies the shuttle from the flight deck on the upper level. The flight deck's control panel has more than 2,000 switches, dials, and displays. That is more than 100 times more controls than the average car has.

The crew lives and works on the lower level, called the mid-deck. The bathroom, sleeping bunks, and kitchen are on the mid-deck. The mid-deck also

Shuttles aren't very roomy, but they can be comfortable for the astronauts to work and live in for a few days.

has storage under the floor panels and lockers for food and other supplies.

In the back of the mid-deck is an airtight room called the air lock. This is where astronauts change into their space suits. To walk in space, an astronaut moves from the air lock through a sealed passage to the payload bay.

After the astronauts change into their space suits, they are ready to go outside of the shuttle.

Astronauts must anchor themselves so they won't fly into space. The foot of the astronaut in the center of this photograph is attached to the shuttle's long arm. The astronaut is lifting a part for the Hubble Space Telescope out of the shuttle payload bay.

The payload bay is where the shuttle carries its cargo. Cargo can be anything from parts to fix a satellite to equipment for science experiments. When astronauts want to send cargo into space, they open the huge doors in the payload bay.

The *Challenger* Disaster

By 1986, shuttles had orbited Earth more than 2,400 times and traveled about 57 million miles (92 million km). That is enough miles to travel to the Moon and back 118 times!

Shuttle missions seemed so safe that NASA decided to

The crew of the Space Shuttle *Challenger*. Front row, from left to right: Michael Smith, Francis Scobee, Ronald McNair. Back row, from left to right: Ellison Onizuka, Christa McAuliffe, Gregory Jarvis, Judith Resnick.

send a person who did not work for NASA or the military into space for the first time. NASA chose Christa McAuliffe, a teacher from New Hampshire, to be part of the *Challenger* shuttle crew.

Launch day—January 28, 1986—was very cold. The sky was clear, so NASA gave the OK to lift off. About a minute after the *Challenger* lifted off, a huge explosion filled the sky. The shuttle had been torn apart and all seven crew members were killed. The whole world was stunned.

When the *Challenger* exploded, it sent clouds of fuel and gas into the air.

For months, NASA tried to find out what went wrong. Scientists finally figured out that the problem was a tiny rubber

After the *Challenger* disaster, NASA created new safety features and improved the shuttle's equipment. The Space Shuttle *Discovery* launch in 1988 got the U.S. space program back on track.

seal called an O-ring. O-rings work well in normal weather, but the cold temperature on that January morning damaged an O-ring. When the shuttle was in the air, gases leaked out and exploded.

After the *Challenger* disaster, NASA worked to make the shuttle safer. However, on February 1, 2003, the Space Shuttle *Columbia* broke apart on its return to Earth.

The Shuttle and the Space Station

At this moment, pieces of an odd-looking building are floating about 240 miles (386 km) above Earth. They are parts for the International Space Station. Sixteen countries are working together to build the station.

The International Space Station is well on its way to being complete. Many shuttle missions take supplies and equipment to the floating construction site.

For the next few years, Space Shuttle missions will transport science equipment, laptop computers, clothing, cameras, and other items to the station. Astronauts will have to make

more than 160 space walks to
put all the pieces together.
When the station is finished,
it will have six research labora-
tories and four full-time crew

This computer-generated image shows
what the International Space Station
will look like when it is complete.

members from countries around the world. A new shuttlelike lifeboat will be kept at the space station in case the crew needs to make emergency repairs or head back to Earth.

The people on the space station will perform science experiments to learn more about Earth, the other planets, and the stars. None of this could happen without the Space Shuttle.

Just think of all the important jobs that Space Shuttles have done!

To Find Out More

These places are great for more information about the Space Shuttle.

Books

Bergin, Mark. **Space Shuttle.** Franklin Watts, 1999.

Bondar, Barbara. **On the Shuttle: Eight Days in Space.** Firefly Books, 1999.

Campbell, Peter A. **Launch Day.** Millbrook, 1995.

Cole, Michael D. **Challenger: America's Space Tragedy.** Enslow, 1995.

———. **Columbia: First Flight of the Space Shuttle.** Enslow, 1995.

Hawcock, David. **Amazing Pop-Up, Pull-Out Space Shuttle.** DK Publishing, 1998.

Langille, Jacqueline and Bobbie Kalman. **The Space Shuttle.** Crabtree, 1998.

Organizations and Online Sites

National Aeronautics and Space Administration (NASA)

http://www.nasa.gov/qanda/space_shuttle.html

This page includes information and questions about past and current shuttle missions.

http://www.nasa.gov

This site is full of recent space news, and links to a NASA for Kids site with cool activities.

http://spaceflight.nasa.gov/

This site has information about the Space Shuttle and the International Space Station.

http://spacelink.nasa.gov

This online library has all kinds of space information.

National Air and Space Museum

Smithsonian Institution
601 Independence Ave. SW
Washington, DC 20560
http://www.nasm.si.edu/

Visit the museum's great website for information about exhibits and special programs.

Space Shuttle Clickable Map

http://seds.lpl.arizona.edu/ssa/docs/Space.Shuttle/

Besides learning general information about the Space Shuttle, you can click on a picture to learn more about its parts.

Important Words

astronaut a person who travels in space

cargo materials carried by a spacecraft, airplane, or ship

engineer a person who uses science to design and build things

mission a special job

orbit to travel around an object, such as a planet

payload bay a compartment on the space shuttle used to for carry cargo, such as satellites, into space

reusable able to be used more than once

wingspan the distance from the tip of one wing to the tip of the other wing

Index

Meet the Author

Allison Lassieur is the author of more than a dozen books for young readers about health, history, world cultures, current events, and American Indians. She also writes biographies and other articles for such magazines as *Disney Adventures*, *Scholastic News*, *Highlights for Children*, and *National Geographic World*.

When Ms. Lassieur is not writing, she enjoys reading, spinning, and participating in historical reenactments.